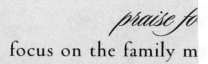

This marriage study series is pure Focus on the Family—
reliable, biblically sound and dedicated to reestablishing family values
in today's society. This series will no doubt help a multitude of couples
strengthen their relationship, not only with each other,
but also with God, the *creator* of marriage itself.

Bruce Wilkinson

Author, The BreakThrough Series: *The Prayer of Jabez,*
Secrets of the Vine and *A Life God Rewards*

In this era of such need, Dr. Dobson's team has produced solid,
helpful materials about Christian marriage. Even if they have been
through marriage studies before, every couple—married or engaged—
will benefit from this foundational study of life together. Thanks to
Focus on the Family for helping set us straight in this top priority.

Charles W. Colson

Chairman, Prison Fellowship Ministries

In my 31 years as a pastor, I've officiated at hundreds of weddings.
Unfortunately, many of those unions failed. I only wish the *Focus on the
Family Marriage Series* had been available to me during those years.
What a marvelous tool you as pastors and Christian leaders have
at your disposal. I encourage you to use it to assist those you
serve in building successful, healthy marriages.

H. B. London, Jr.

Vice President, Ministry Outreach/Pastoral Ministries
Focus on the Family

Looking for a prescription for a better marriage?
You'll enjoy this timely and practical series!

Dr. Kevin Leman

Author, *Sheet Music: Uncovering the Secrets of
Sexual Intimacy in Marriage*

The *Focus on the Family Marriage Series* is successful because it shifts
the focus from how to fix or strengthen a marriage to *who* can do it.
Through this study you will learn that a blessed marriage will be the
happy by-product of a closer relationship with the *creator* of marriage.

Lisa Whelchel

Author, *Creative Correction* and
The Facts of Life and Other Lessons My Father Taught Me

In a day and age where the covenant of marriage is so quickly tossed
aside in the name of incompatibility and irreconcilable differences, a
marriage Bible study that is both inspirational and practical is desperately
needed. The *Focus on the Family Marriage Series* is what couples are seeking.
I give my highest recommendation to this Bible study series that has the
potential to dramatically impact and improve marriages today. Marriage
is not so much about finding the right partner as it is about being the
right partner. These studies give wonderful biblical teachings for
helping those who want to learn the beautiful art of being and
becoming all that God intends in their marriage.

Lysa TerKeurst

President, Proverbs 31 Ministries
Author, *Capture His Heart* and *Capture Her Heart*

focus on the family® marriage series

the . .
surprising
marriage

Gospel Light

Gospel Light is an evangelical Christian publisher dedicated to serving the local church. We believe God's vision for Gospel Light is to provide church leaders with biblical, user-friendly materials that will help them evangelize, disciple and minister to children, youth and families.

It is our prayer that this Gospel Light resource will help you discover biblical truth for your own life and help you minister to others. May God richly bless you.

For a free catalog of resources from Gospel Light, please call your Christian supplier or contact us at 1-800-4-GOSPEL *or* www.gospellight.com

PUBLISHING STAFF
William T. Greig, Chairman
Kyle Duncan, Publisher
Dr. Elmer L. Towns, Senior Consulting Publisher
Pam Weston, Senior Editor
Patti Pennington Virtue, Associate Editor
Hilary Young, Editorial Assistant
Jessie Minassian, Editorial Assistant
Bayard Taylor, M.Div., Senior Editor, Biblical and Theological Issues
Samantha A. Hsu, Cover and Internal Designer
Tom Stephen and **Virginia Starkey,** Contributing Writers

ISBN 0-8307-3153-9
© 2003 Focus on the Family
All rights reserved.
Printed in the U.S.A.

table of contents

foreword

The most urgent mission field on Earth is not across the sea or even across the street—it's right where you live: in your home and family. Jesus' last instruction was to "make disciples of all nations" (Matthew 28:19). At the thought of this command, our eyes look across the world for our work field. That's not bad; it's just not *all*. God intended the home to be the first place of Christian discipleship and growth (see Deuteronomy 6:4-8). Our family members must be the *first* ones we reach out to in word and example with the gospel of the Lord Jesus Christ, and the fundamental way in which this occurs is through the marriage relationship.

Divorce, blended families, the breakdown of communication and the complexities of daily life are taking a devastating toll on the God-ordained institutions of marriage and family. We do not need to look hard or search far for evidence that even Christian marriages and families are also in a desperate state. In response to the need to build strong Christ-centered marriages and families, this series was developed.

Focus on the Family is well known and respected worldwide for its stead-fast dedication to preserving the sanctity of marriage and family life. I can think of no better partnership than the one formed by Focus on the Family and Gospel Light to produce the *Focus on the Family Marriage Series*. This series is well-written, biblically sound and right on target for guiding couples to explore the foundation God has laid for marriage and to see Him as the role model for the perfect spouse. Through these studies, seeds will be planted that will germinate in your heart and mind for many years to come.

In our practical, bottom-line culture, we often want to jump over the *why* and get straight to the *what*. We think that by *doing* the six steps or *learning* the five ways, we will reach the goal. But deep-rooted growth is slower and more purposeful and begins with a well-grounded understanding of God's divine design. Knowing why marriage exists is crucial to making the how-tos more effective. Marriage is a gift from God, a unique and distinct covenant relationship through which His glory and goodness can resonate, and it is only through knowing the architect and His plan that we will build our marriage on the surest foundation.

God created marriage; He has a specific purpose for it, and He is committed to filling with fresh life and renewed strength each union yielded to Him. God wants to gather the hearts of every couple together, unite them in love and walk them to the finish line—all in His great grace and goodness.

May God, in His grace, lead you into His truth, strengthening your lives and your marriage.

Gary T. Smalley
Founder and Chairman of the Board
Smalley Relationship Center

introduction

*At the beginning of creation God "made them male and female." "For this
reason a man will leave his father and mother and be united to his wife,
and the two will become one flesh." So they are no longer two, but one.*
Mark 10:6-8

The Surprising Marriage can be used in a variety of situations, including small-group Bible studies, Sunday School classes or counseling or mentoring situations. An individual couple can also use this book as an at-home marriage-building study.

Each of the four sessions contains four main components.

Session Overview

Tilling the Ground
This is an introduction to the topic being discussed—commentary and questions to direct your thoughts toward the main idea of the session.

Planting the Seed
This is the Bible study portion in which you will read Scripture and answer questions to help discover lasting truths from God's Word.

Watering the Hope
This is a time for discussion and prayer. Whether you are using the study at home as a couple, in a small group or in a classroom setting, talking about the lesson with your spouse is a great way to solidify the truth and plant it deeply into your hearts.

Harvesting the Fruit
As a point of action, this portion of the session offers suggestions on putting the truth of the Word into action in your marriage relationship.

Suggestions for Individual Couple Study

There are at least three options for using this study as a couple.

- It may be used as a devotional study that each spouse would study individually through the week; then on a specified day, come together and discuss what you have learned and how to apply it to your marriage.
- You might choose to study one session together in an evening and then work on the application activities during the rest of the week.
- Because of the short length of this study, it is a great resource for a weekend retreat. Take a trip away for the weekend, and study each session together, interspersed with your favorite leisure activities.

Suggestions for Group Study

There are many ways that this study can be used in a group situation. The most common way is in a small-group Bible study format. However, it can also be used in adult Sunday School class. However you choose to use it, there are some general guidelines to follow for group study.

- Keep the group small—five to six couples is probably the maximum.
- Ask couples to commit to regular attendance for the four weeks of the study. Regular attendance is a key to building relationships and trust in a group.
- Encourage participants *not* to share anything of a personal or potentially embarrassing nature without first asking the spouse's permission.
- Whatever is discussed in the group meetings is to be held in strictest confidence among group members only.

There are additional leader helps in the back of this book and in *The Focus on the Family Marriage Ministry Guide*.

Suggestions for Mentoring or Counseling Relationships

This study also lends itself for use in relationships where one couple mentors or counsels another couple.

- A mentoring relationship, where a couple that has been married for several years is assigned to meet on a regular basis with a younger couple, could be arranged through a system set up by a church or ministry.
- A less formal way to start a mentoring relationship is for a younger couple to take the initiative and approach a couple that exemplify a mature, godly marriage and ask them to meet with them on a regular basis. Or the reverse might be a mature couple that approaches a younger couple to begin a mentoring relationship.
- When asked to mentor, some might shy away and think that they could never do that, knowing that their own marriage is less than perfect. But just as we are to disciple new believers, we must learn to disciple married couples to strengthen marriages in this difficult world. The Lord has promised to be "with you always" (Matthew 28:20).
- Before you begin to mentor a couple, first complete the study yourselves. This will serve to strengthen your own marriage and prepare you for leading another couple.
- Be prepared to learn as much or more than the couple(s) you will mentor.

There are additional helps for mentoring relationships in *The Focus on the Family Marriage Ministry Guide*.

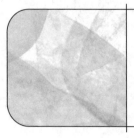

The Focus on the Family Marriage Series *is based on Al Janssen's* The Marriage Masterpiece *(Wheaton, IL: Tyndale House Publishers, 2001), an insightful look at what marriage can—and should—be. In this study, we are pleased to lead you through the wonderful journey of discovering the joy in your marriage that God wants you to experience!*

a faith journey *together*

God blessed them and said to them, "Be fruitful and increase in number; fill the earth and subdue it. Rule over the fish of the sea and the birds of the air and over every living creature that moves on the ground."

Genesis 1:28

In your marriage, do you and your spouse operate more like James Bond, Agent 007, in the movies or the goofy characters in the classic *Road to . . .* movies starring Bing Crosby and Bob Hope?

James Bond is Hollywood's version of a rugged individualist who operates primarily on his own. At the end of each movie, there is no doubt who is responsible for saving the world.

The Bing Crosby and Bob Hope characters were on a mission together (albeit as con men!). While they had their disagreements, there was no doubt that only when they worked together could they accomplish what they set out to do.

God designed marriage so that we might experience a surprising, joyous adventure sharing a common mission and purpose. While you may offer support for your spouse's dreams and desires, it is important also to share the purpose God has given you as a couple.

Let's explore the differences between an occupation and a vocation.

A person's occupation is all that he or she does to provide for his or her family. Whether you work outside the home or work at home, what you do to provide for yourself and your household is your occupation. A person's vocation is the divine purpose or job given by God in which he or she finds joy and satisfaction. The apostle Paul's occupation was making tents—his vocation was as a missionary primarily to non-Jews.

Our culture often places great value on a person's occupation, focusing on money, fame and power as measures of success. God, on the other hand, values a person's vocation. If your occupation and your vocation involve the same work, you are most fortunate. Many people, however, have an occupation that simply provides the means to accomplish their vocation.

1. How do you feel about your occupation?

    How does your spouse feel about his or her occupation?

2. What is your vocation? What do you do that brings joy to your life and contributes to God's work in the world?

3. If you have a hard time identifying a vocation, what would you like or imagine your vocation to be?

4. On a scale of 1 to 10, how well do you and your spouse share with each other your dreams and hopes for serving Christ together?

1	2	3	4	5	6	7	8	9	10
Never			Occasionally			Often			All the time

While most of us will not share a common occupation with our spouse, we are called to have a shared vocation, a purpose that God wants us to accomplish—this is part of the process of becoming one in marriage. When we take time to discover what God has in store for our marriage, we will find that our marriage and our relationship with God will grow and mature like a well-watered tree as described in Psalm 1.

planting the seed

As you read about the creation of human beings in Genesis 1 and 2, listen for what these passages tell you about God, about people and about the blessing or plan God has for a married couple sharing a vocation together.

Knowing God

As you read Genesis 1:26-31, notice that God describes Himself using the pronoun "us."

5. Why would the writer of Genesis—who believed that God is one—write that God used a word that indicates He is more than one person?

6. According to Genesis 1:2, who was hovering?

7. As described in John 1:1, who is the Word?

8. Based on Genesis 1:1-5 and John 1:1-5, who is the "us" of creation in Genesis 1:26-31?

While we may not fully understand the deep mysteries of the Trinity, there are some things we can understand. First, God is one. Second, God has been revealed in three different ways: Father, Son, Holy Spirit. Third, all three aspects of God are necessary. In God's very nature, one being exists in relationship: three are one.

9. How might this three-way relationship in the Trinity relate to the shared purpose in a marriage relationship?

Knowing People

God created human beings in His own image. Just as God exists in relationship, we were made to exist in relationship with one another and with Him.

10. What difference should it make in our lives that the image of God incorporates both male and female characteristics?

11. What does Genesis 2:24 tell us about the relationship between a husband and wife?

In what ways have you experienced being one with your spouse in your relationship?

In what areas do you need to work harder at becoming one?

Knowing God's Blessing

12. How does God bless the couple in Genesis 1:28-31?

How does His blessing suggest a shared vocation?

13. When have you experienced the joy of doing something with your spouse that you both felt God had called you to do?

14. According to Genesis 3:16-19, what happened to the shared vocation when sin entered into the picture?

15. Is it possible to operate in separate ministry arenas and still share in the vocation of your spouse? Explain.

16. Describe a time when you thought you were following God's plan only to find out that you were following your own desires and felt separated from your spouse. Why do you think that happened?

A Biblical Model

In Acts 18, we are introduced to a married couple who knew the joy of sharing a common mission: Priscilla and Aquila.

17. What do each of the following verses tell you about this amazing Christian couple?

    Acts 18:1-3

Acts 18:18-21

Acts 18:24-28

Romans 16:3

1 Corinthians 16:19

2 Timothy 4:19

18. What do we know about these two as individuals regarding their differences and similarities?

What was their shared vocation?

19. What does this brief study of Priscilla and Aquila tell us about the purpose of a Christ-centered marriage?

20. Do you know a Priscilla-and-Aquila couple? Describe how they demonstrate to you what it means to have a shared vocation.

Priscilla and Aquila give us a wonderful picture of a married couple with a shared vocation. While the Scriptures don't tell us everything about this couple (surely they had their disagreements) what we do know is that they model for us what a Christian marriage might look like.

watering the hope

When we walk closely with our spouse, sharing a vocation and being faithful to God together, we are truly becoming one in our marriage.

Having a shared vocation goes against the current trend in our culture—most of us have been raised to be independent. While independence is important in some areas, as a married couple we are called to be neither dependent nor independent. Rather, we are called to be *interdependent*—each playing a critical role in one another's life and in a shared vocation.

21. List some ways that a married couple can begin the process of sharing a vocation together.

22. What fears or obstacles do you have about sharing a vocation with your spouse?

In what ways can you overcome your fears or obstacles?

23. Thinking about a Priscilla-and-Aquila couple, what joys do you see as they share a common God-directed purpose?

harvesting the fruit

Having a shared vocation means actively following God's will to serve in this world as a team. Consider the different ways you want to follow God's call both individually and together.

24. What are your spiritual gifts and natural talents, or abilities?

What are your spouse's spiritual gifts and natural talents, or abilities?

25. What outside resources (i.e., finances, location, connections, etc.) has God given to you and your spouse that you could use for serving others?

26. How would you like to follow God's call?

27. How can you and your spouse follow God's call together?

Make a date to pray at least twice a week with your spouse so that God may continue to shape your shared vocation. Realize that even if you and your spouse are not on the same page, prayer and Bible study will enable God to mold and shape your heart to His plan for your marriage.

We plan to pray together on _____ at _____.

We plan to talk together about our shared vocation on _____ at _____.

passing on the legacy

I have been reminded of your sincere faith, which first lived in your grandmother Lois and in your mother Eunice and, I am persuaded, now lives in you also.

2 Timothy 1:5

Whether your parents were (or are) happily married or divorced, much of your understanding of marriage came as you witnessed their relationship. While your understanding of marriage began with your parents, it doesn't end there. You've been watching others and learning about marriage your entire life. No doubt you've seen couples who care for one another and couples who spend most of their time tearing each other apart.

The frightening—and wonderful—part of your adventure in marriage is that others are watching you. Whether you're newly married or whether you've recently celebrated your fiftieth anniversary, you're passing on a legacy of marriage to those around you through your actions and words.

What kind of inheritance do you want to pass on to the next generation? The best inheritance you can give your children and others is the model of a Christ-lived marriage.

tilling the ground

Let's consider the impact of marriage models on your own marriage.

1. What positive aspects of marriage did your parents demonstrate that you would like to continue in your own marriage?

    What, if any, aspects would you *not* want to continue in your marriage?

2. How do you see Christlike behavior modeled in the marriages of others?

3. Of the different marriages you've watched over the years—other than that of your parents—which one has had the biggest impact on you (either positively or negatively)?

In his letter to the Romans, Paul wrote, "And we know that in all things God works for the good of those who love him, who have been called according to his purpose" (Romans 8:28). God is able to take all we've inherited—the good and the bad—and use it for good. As you express your love for God and as you submit to Him and follow His design, God can transform your heart, mind and marriage into His perfect design.

King Solomon knew something about how to build a house. Not only did he build a wonderful house for himself and his family, but he was also given the opportunity to build God's house—the first temple in Jerusalem.

4. How does Psalm 127:1-2 relate to building a marriage?

5. If others were to look at your marriage, which of the following road signs would best describe your marriage? Explain your choice.

☐ God at Work
☐ Watch for Falling Rocks
☐ Divided Road Ahead
☐ Rough Road
☐ Other _____

Building the Right Foundation

Jesus also knew a thing or two about building a house as we read at the end of the Sermon on the Mount in the Gospel of Matthew.

6. In Matthew 7:24-27, what did the two builders in this parable have in common?

In what ways were the builders different from each other?

7. What kinds of things, ideas or attitudes might contribute to a foundation of sand in a marriage?

What—along with being Christ-centered—might be included in the rock foundation of a marriage?

The best legacy we can pass on to others is a life that not only hears the words of Jesus but also puts them into practice (see James 2:14,18,26).

Building a Legacy

How can we build a marriage that is Christ-lived? How can we cultivate an atmosphere and attitude that build up our spouse? We will be turning back to Jesus' words in the Gospel of Matthew, as Jesus begins His Sermon on the Mount.

Atmosphere

Read Matthew 5:3-10. Each of these statements begins with the same word—"blessed." A translation of this could be "happy"—but only if we clearly understand that Jesus is not talking about a *feeling*; He is talking about a *condition* of life. It is only in following His commands that an atmosphere of being blessed, or happy, will surround your house.

8. What word or phrase would best describe the atmosphere of your marriage?

What aspects of your marriage are a blessing for you?

Attitude

Traditionally, Christians have referred to the words of Jesus in Matthew 5:3-10 as the Beatitudes. Jesus gives us a way to live by showing us right attitudes. Let's investigate what attitudes will help us create an inheritance worth passing on.

"Blessed are the poor in spirit, for theirs is the kingdom of heaven" (Matthew 5:3). Another translation of this verse reads, "You're blessed when you're at the end of your rope. With less of you there is more of God and his rule" (*THE MESSAGE*).

9. Have you ever been in a situation in which you felt you were at the end of your rope? How did you react?

10. How would an attitude of knowing that God is in control change the way you look at your problems?

"Blessed are those who mourn, for they will be comforted" (Matthew 5:4). Acknowledging the losses that occur in our marriage gives us the freedom to be honest with our pain and grief. When we are honest with our pain and grief, we are freed up to experience the joy and comfort that God and our spouse can give to us. This is an awesome inheritance to give our children and others in our sphere of influence.

11. What are some losses (i.e., a job, a loved one, a move, etc.) that you and/or your spouse have experienced since you have been married?

How did you handle the situation? How did your spouse help you handle the situation?

What blessing have you experienced as a result of this situation?

"Blessed are the meek, for they will inherit the earth" (Matthew 5:5). To be meek means to be have a right attitude about who you are—not too high an estimation and not too low an estimation of yourself—in other words, an attitude of humility.

12. What would an attitude of humbleness in marriage look like?

How do you need to express humility in your marriage?

"Blessed are those who hunger and thirst for righteousness, for they will be filled" (Matthew 5:6). Whether you are just beginning to understand the concept of righteousness or whether you and your spouse have been seeking it for a long time, Jesus promises that if you desire it, you will receive it. Simply put, to be righteous is to be in a right standing with God.

13. Do you have a hunger, or desire, to be right with God? If so, have you shared that desire with your spouse and your family? If not, what kills your hunger, or desire, for God?

How might a hunger for righteousness be manifested in a marriage?

"Blessed are the merciful, for they will be shown mercy" (Matthew 5:7). Mercy expresses care for those in need. A friend recently shared about a time when she was talking about the difficult problems she was having caring for her aging mother. As she talked, she found herself complaining about some of the menial tasks. When she looked up, she realized that her son was listening very intently. She then imagined that one day she would be in a nursing home and her son would be the one taking care of her. Suddenly, her attitude changed.

14. How can mercy be shown in a marriage relationship?

"Blessed are the pure in heart, for they will see God" (Matthew 5:8). Another translation states it this way: "You're blessed when you get your inside world—your mind and heart—put right. Then you can see God in the outside world" (*THE MESSAGE*).

15. How might a pure, or right, heart be demonstrated in a marriage?

**"Blessed are the peacemakers, for they will be called sons of God"
(Matthew 5:9).** Jesus is not talking about peace at any cost. The peace of
Jesus is not simply the absence of conflict but rather a peace that comes
when people put the interests of others above their own interests and needs
(see Philippians 2:4).

16. How can we be peacemakers in and through our marriage?

**"Blessed are those who are persecuted because of righteousness, for
theirs is the kingdom of heaven" (Matthew 5:10).** Have you ever done the
right thing, felt good about it and still had people give you grief about your
attitude or actions? Jesus explains that if we follow Him, we will experience
resistance and even out-and-out persecution.

17. What resistance have you experienced in trying to follow God's plan in
your marriage?

What type of legacy are you passing on to others when they see your
response to difficult times and people?

Now that we've looked at the atmosphere and attitudes Jesus expects of
us in our life and in our marriage, let's turn our attention to the actions He
may be asking us to take.

As you studied the words of Jesus, were you inspired or overwhelmed? God's truth is not easy to live out in everyday life. If you are feeling a bit over-whelmed, you are in the right spot. Remember: Jesus began by saying, "Blessed are the poor in spirit" (Matthew 5:3). Acknowledging that you need His help is the first step. Our hope does not come from *our own* ability, but from *God's* ability to bring about a good work to "those who love him" and are "called according to his purpose" (Romans 8:28). How do you water this hope? By turning over your life and your marriage to Jesus Christ.

18. Why is it difficult to turn every aspect of your life and marriage over to God?

19. Select from the following statements the one that best describes where you are in trusting God with your life and marriage. After you've selected your statement, take a moment to discuss your choice with your spouse.

   ☐ I have never made a commitment to follow Jesus Christ. I work hard to make a good marriage, but I don't understand how to give my life and marriage to Christ. (Please contact your pastor, group leader or a Christian friend to help you understand the process of committing your life and marriage to Jesus Christ.)
   ☐ I've followed Jesus in the past but have not been close to Him recently.
   ☐ I am following Christ in some areas of my life and want to com-pletely trust Him with my marriage and every aspect of my life.

Whether you are just beginning to understand who Jesus Christ is and how to follow Him or you are well on the way to trusting Jesus with everything in your life, know that God is waiting for you to turn to Him (see Luke 15:1-23). He wants you to ask for forgiveness for the sins of your past and to find strength through Him for living today and all of your tomorrows.

As we turn to God and trust Him completely, He will transform the atmosphere of our marriage and our attitudes, and He will begin to work on changing our actions. He has promised to continue the work He has begun in you (see Philippians 1:6).

 harvesting the fruit

Once we've placed ourselves in God's hands, it is time to start putting His words into action. As we put into practice the words of Jesus, we will begin to see tangible results! The following inventory will help you begin to take practical steps toward creating a household that is blessed. As you work through this exercise, avoid telling your spouse how he or she can improve—instead, think through which actions you can take as a couple.

Putting the Be-Attitudes into Action Inventory

On a scale of 1 to 10, rate the atmosphere in your marriage for each of the 10 beatitudes from Matthew 5; then answer the question that follows each characteristic.

20. "Blessed are the poor in spirit" (v. 3).
    _____ *My marriage has an atmosphere of dependence on God.*
    What is one step you and your spouse can take to actively depend on God in your marriage?

21. "Blessed are those who mourn" (v. 4).

    _____ *My marriage has an atmosphere of being able to grieve openly.*

    How can you and your spouse better share your grief and sorrows with one another?

22. "Blessed are the meek" (v. 5).

    _____ *My marriage has an atmosphere of humility.*

    In what area do you and your spouse need to grow in humility as a couple?

23. "Blessed are those who hunger and thirst for righteousness" (v. 6).

    _____ *My marriage has an atmosphere of desiring God.*

    What is one step you and your spouse can take to seek after God as a couple?

24. "Blessed are the merciful" (v. 7).

    _____ *My marriage has an atmosphere of mercy.*

    How can you and your spouse cultivate an atmosphere of mercy and forgiveness in your home?

25. "Blessed are the pure in heart" (v. 8).

_____ *My marriage has an atmosphere of protecting the purity of my heart and the heart of my spouse.*

What is one step you and your spouse can take to better protect the purity of your hearts?

26. "Blessed are the peacemakers" (v. 9).

_____ *My marriage has an atmosphere of peacemaking during times of conflict.*

How can you and your spouse exemplify peacemaking through your marriage?

27. "Blessed are those who are persecuted because of righteousness" (v. 10).

_____ *My marriage reflects a commitment to follow God regardless of worldly influences.*

In what area can you and your spouse better stand firm in following God's will for your marriage?

If you fail to plan, you plan to fail—this is especially true when it comes to passing on a legacy. Making these characteristics stand out in your marriage will take time. Set up a time to meet with your spouse (and your children if they are old enough) to talk about these characteristics on a regular basis. The following are a few suggestions:

- Once a week, take some time before or after a meal to evaluate progress on one action step that you planned to take.
- Once a month on a date, take the entire time to review where you are in putting these attitudes into practice.
- Encourage each other to memorize these first 10 verses of Matthew 5 to remind you of the steps you plan to take.

understanding and *celebrating* differences

The body is a unit, though it is made up many parts; and though all its parts are many, they form one body. So it is with Christ.

1 Corinthians 12:12

A friend of mine asked me recently, "Do you know the first joke in the Bible?"

"No," I answered.

She responded, "God made them male and female and then expected them to get along."

"Irreconcilable differences" is a common phrase used on a divorce petition in a no-fault-divorce state. It is a fact: Women and men *are* different. We have different ways of thinking, communicating, expressing sexuality—the list goes on and on. Simply put, God wired us differently *on purpose*. Add to this our upbringing, life experience and myriad other factors and it's no wonder we might have irreconcilable differences!

Here's the good news. Our differences are not irreconcilable. In fact, God intends for our differences to enhance our marriage, not destroy it. As you begin to understand the differences between you and your spouse and to enjoy those differences, God can bring a depth and excitement to your marriage that you might not think possible. While understanding and enjoying our differences does take work, listening to God's Word and allowing Him to work through us will take His design (male and female) and create a masterpiece using the wide variety of colors between you (your differences) to paint with.

tilling the ground

The differences between husbands and wives have become a rich source of hilarious material for television sitcoms and romantic comedy movies. Not only do we have to deal with gender differences, but there may be personality, family, cultural and educational differences to deal with as well. In fact, with so many factors involved, it is surprising that any of us stay married!

1. What are some of the basic differences between men and women?

   Do you find these differences fascinating, funny or frustrating? Explain.

2. Describe some of the differences between you and your spouse that have surprised you.

God made us "male and female" (Genesis 1:27) for a purpose. Let's discover and celebrate those differences.

Although the first chapter of Genesis tells us that God created both man and woman in His image, it doesn't tell us *why* God created them male and female. The second chapter of Genesis provides some insight into why God made us different.

3. According to Genesis 2:18-20, what actions did God take first before creating a helper for Adam and why do you think He did these things?

| It's a Fact! | *It's a Fact! The word translated as "helper" is ezer in Hebrew. This word doesn't refer to a servant or a lesser creature to be ruled but, rather, to one who will add something that the one being helped does not possess. Within the Hebrew Scriptures, God is often referred to as our helper—our ezer.[1]* |

4. What do each of the following verses say about God as our helper?

Exodus 18:4

Psalm 33:20

Psalm 46:1

Hebrews 13:6

5. In what ways have you experienced God as the one who helps you?

6. According to Genesis 2:21-25, what is it about the woman that makes her the perfect complement (or helper) to the man?

   How do the man's words in verse 23 reflect how he views the woman?

7. What appreciation do you gain about the differences between men and women from God's original design and intent?

We Need Variety

In order to better understand God's grand design for men and women being different and yet one in marriage, let's turn our attention to Paul's letter to the Corinthians. Read Paul's description of what love means in 1 Corinthians 13:1-8.

8. How might this passage relate to a husband and wife loving each other and accepting their differences?

9. As you read 1 Corinthians 12:12-26, consider how Paul's metaphor of the body illustrates the reasons behind God's design for the differences in spouses.

10. What might happen to the Church (or a marriage) if there were no variety in its members (see vv. 14-16)?

11. Describe how the differences between spouses can add a sense of completeness to a marriage.

We Each Have Different Functions

God has designed each of us with different gifts and skills. In order for the body to function as God intended, each part must perform its function.

12. According to 1 Corinthians 12:17-20,27-31, why is it important for the Church to incorporate the different gifts and skills of its members?

How might your marriage be different or what would be lacking if you and your spouse had exactly the same gifts and skills?

We Each Have Value

Just as parts of the body have value simply because the body would not work as God intended unless all the parts are in working order, so it is with our different functions in the Body of Christ.

13. Read 1 Corinthians 12:21-26. How can individuals show that they value their spouse?

What is one area in which you can improve in showing respect to your spouse's role in your marriage?

 watering the hope

Let's reconsider the Bible passages we've been studying and apply them specifically to your marriage.

Variety Is Necessary for Completeness

Answer the following questions honestly (i.e., don't write the answers that you think that your spouse wants to hear!). It's perfectly OK to have different views in your marriage; the important thing is finding out where you stand so that you can combine your views to create a partnership that works for both of you.

14. What is your idea of a perfect night out?

15. What is the best way to save money?

What is the best way to spend money?

16. How important is sexual intimacy to you?

17. How important is talk time in your marriage?

18. What is your definition of a clean house?

19. How much affection is enough?

20. What is the best way to discipline children?

21. Describe the ideal vacation.

Share your answers to these questions with your spouse. **Note:** Expect your answers to be different—and remember, that's OK! We can celebrate our differences by taking time to see situations through the eyes of our spouse. As much as we hate to admit it, no one has all the right answers. And there is more than one way to do most things. As you begin to understand the way your spouse thinks and you give validation to variations, you are on your way to celebrating those differences.

22. For those questions you and your spouse answered differently, what is good about the way your *spouse* thinks? (This will need to be answered after you and your spouse have shared your answers to questions 14 to 21.)

23. Reread 1 Corinthians 13:1-8. How can these verses help you begin to enjoy the differences between yourself and your spouse?

Different Gifts and Skills Produce Uniqueness

24. In the left column, list the gifts and skills you bring to your marriage; in the right column, list those that your spouse brings.

My Gifts and Skills	My Spouse's Gifts and Skills

How do these gifts and skills work to complement each other?

Are any of these gifts and/or skills sources of competition or friction between you and your spouse? Explain.

Uniqueness Is Valued

We demonstrate what we value by the amount of time, emotions and actions we invest. How you respond to the differences between yourself and your spouse is an indicator of whether or not you value your spouse and his or her unique gifts and skills.

25. In what ways do you demonstrate value in your spouse through your time, emotions and actions?

One step toward understanding and enjoying the distinctive characteristics of your spouse is to listen to his or her love language.[2] This means observing how he or she expresses love to others—an indicator of the way a person would like to be valued or respected. More often than not, our spouse's love language will be different from ours.

26. Describe what you would need from your spouse in order to feel valued by him or her.

Have you ever received a gift that the giver absolutely loved and you wondered, *Why in the world would anyone buy this gift for me?* The best way to know what your spouse needs is simply to ask and then begin to think through the steps you can take to express love to him or her in the appropriate love language.

 harvesting the fruit

Are you ready to put into practice some of what you've learned thus far? You can use the following action steps to help you grow in many areas of your marriage. Discuss them and decide with your spouse one area in your marriage that you would like to work on over the next two weeks, and apply these steps to that one area. As you begin this process, make a commitment to read 1 Corinthians 12 and 13 once a day as you begin to better understand and celebrate your differences.

Action Step One—Choose an area in which you and your spouse think differently. *For example: The importance and amount of time showing affection.*

Action Step Two—Become a student of your spouse for the next week. Take a week to study how your spouse thinks about this area of life. This week is not a time to discuss but a time to study. Set aside your preconceived ideas—and start taking notes. You may even want to start a notebook to write down what you learn each day. *For example: What does my spouse mean by affection? How did his (her) family express affection? How did he (she) feel about that? How does he (she) show affection for others outside the family?*

Action Step Three—On the final day, take what you've learned about your spouse and clarify what you've learned from him or her. *For example: Talk with your spouse about what you understood concerning his or her need to feel affection.*

Action Step Four—Put into practice what you have learned. Simply put, do what your spouse said. You will have a time to discuss what works for you in this process, but before you do that, simply try to respond specifically to what you've learned about your spouse.

Action Step Five—At the end of two weeks, set aside time to discuss what you've learned and experienced over the last two weeks. You might want to talk about what has been surprising and frustrating.

Important! Be sure to begin and end your discussion of these action steps with prayer!

Notes

1. Victor P. Hamilton, *The New International Commentary on the Old Testament: The Book of Genesis, Chapters 1-17* (Grand Rapids, MI: William Eerdmans Publishing Company, 1990), p. 176.

2. For more information about love languages, read Gary Chapman, *The Five Love Languages* (Chicago: Northfield Publishers, 1992).

living out
the master plan

I am the vine; you are the branches. If a man remains in me and I in him,
he will bear much fruit; apart from me you can do nothing.
John 15:5

Read the following completely different views of marriage, both of which were shared by grown children about their parents' marriages:

"I really don't trust the institution of marriage," my friend said as we talked about his future.

"Why is that?" I asked.

"Well, my mom and dad stopped loving each other a long time ago. They have lived in the same house for 30 years, but I don't remember the last time I saw them talking about anything important. They put up with each other. Actually, I think they stayed together for us, the kids. But to be honest, I think their staying together gave me a worse impression of marriage than if they had broken up."

I talked with a woman during a premarital counseling session and she had this to say about her parents when asked what she liked about their marriage: "I love to see my mom and dad together. They are like best friends. They enjoy being with each other and they have such a good way of caring for each other. Sure, they're not perfect, but I have never doubted that they genuinely cared for and loved each other."

What makes the difference between the two views and the marriages they represent? These marriages were similar in the fact that both couples remained married. However, the grown children of these two couples revealed the truth: One of the marriages spoke of life, the other hovered near death. What made the difference?

God's desire for your marriage is that your relationship would be filled with life—not merely an outward commitment to stay together, but an inward commitment to keep God at the center of your marriage.

tilling the ground

Whether you realize it or not, you are leaving a legacy. The choices you make will determine whether or not your legacy is a worthy one. As you and your spouse journey through this life together, you are developing a legacy and your choices will determine the quality of that legacy.

1. If you knew you were going to die in a month, what would you do and say to the people you care about?

    What wisdom would you want to be sure you passed on to the children in your life? What would you want to leave with them that would impact the rest of their lives?

2. What would you want people to remember about you?

3. What would you hope people would remember about your marriage?

Whatever the content, you would probably be sure to make your words count and pass on what is important to you. Most of us will not have that kind of warning, but we do need to live our lives in such a way that we make them count for eternity.

planting the seed

John 13 relates the events around Jesus' last meal with His disciples. He had important things to share with those He loved before His death on the cross. You may be surprised to find that the same wisdom Jesus passed on to His disciples is the key to leaving a legacy of life, joy and peace through your marriage.

Demonstrating Love

In John 13:1-17, Jesus demonstrated the extent of His love for His disciples.

4. What was Jesus showing His disciples when He washed their feet?

The act of washing the feet of a guest was something that was usually left for a servant to do. In fact, it was considered the lowliest job in a household. Can you imagine what it must have been like to wash the feet of people who wore sandals and walked on dusty roads?

5. What was Peter's first reaction to Jesus' act of washing his feet? What was his second reaction?

How do you react when your spouse seeks to serve you? Are you appreciative, recognizing it as an act of humility and love; do you simply take it for granted, considering that you deserve it; or are you resentful of his or her humble act?

6. In your marriage, what would be the modern-day equivalent of foot washing?

7. How could a married couple demonstrate this servant attitude toward others?

As human beings affected by the Fall, our first inclination is to want to be served—to win the argument, to avoid the chores, to choose the channel to watch—instead of serving others. Fortunately, Jesus recognized that we would need help to serve others and follow Him, so He sent a helper—the Holy Spirit—to aid us.

Bearing Fruit

Without the help of the Holy Spirit, it would be impossible to consistently serve others in a Christlike manner. Read John 14:15-17. The word translated "counselor" is *parakletos* in the original Greek language: *para* meaning "come alongside" and *kletos* meaning "one who is sent."[1] As we follow Christ and trust in Him for love and forgiveness, He has provided the Holy Spirit to "come alongside" and help us.

8. How does the idea of having a counselor, advocate and divine helper impact how you approach service to others?

Let's look at what Scripture has to say about those who follow their own desires and those who allow the Holy Spirit to guide their lives.

9. What does Galatians 5:16-18 say about the results of living by the Spirit?

What is said about living to gratify our own desires?

10. Galatians 5:19-21 lists the acts that result from following one's own desires. Which do you think are most common problems in marriages today?

Which acts are the most common reasons marriages either end in divorce or become stagnant?

11. As you read Galatians 5:22-26, notice that the results of following our own desires are considered acts, but the works of the Spirit are called fruit. What do you think is the significance of that distinction?

12. Which of the fruit of the Spirit do you already experience in your life and marriage?

    Which do you long for?

13. According to verses 24 and 25, how does one experience the fruit of the Spirit?

    In John 15:1-8, Jesus uses the metaphor of a vine to explain how we can live a life that is fruit bearing.

14. What happens to the branch that remains connected to the vine (v. 5)?

Jesus said, "If you remain in me and my words remain in you, ask whatever you wish, and it will be given to you" (v. 7). George R. Beasley-Murray wrote, "To 'remain' in Jesus has a deeper significance than simply to continue to believe in him, although it includes that; it connotes continuing to live in association or in union with him."[2]

15. How would remaining in Jesus affect the desires of a person's heart?

16. What does verse 8 say to you about God's ability to create an environment of life in your marriage?

watering the hope

As you consider the various aspects of demonstrating loving service and bearing spiritual fruit in your personal life, you and your spouse also need to consider how to apply these concepts in your marriage.

Identifying Deadly Choices

Are there areas in your marriage in which you are choosing death by following the acts of the sinful nature as listed in Galatians 5? Review the following list with your spouse and talk about how, if at all, these areas may be influencing your marriage; then decide on one step you can take to begin to work on this area of your relationship:

Drunkenness   Idolatry and witchcraft

Fits of rage   Selfish ambition

Hatred, discord, jealousy or envy   Sexual immorality

Other (explain) _____

17. List three ways in which you would like to start doing a better job at demonstrating love for your spouse.

Identifying Life-Giving Choices

We each must make myriad choices every day—from the mundane to the life changing. What choices are you making to live a life that is connected to Jesus Christ?

18. From the following list of the fruit of the Spirit, choose which three you would most like to see in your life:

☐ Love   ☐ Joy

☐ Peace   ☐ Patience

☐ Kindness   ☐ Goodness

☐ Faithfulness   ☐ Self-control

19. Rate yourself and your marriage using the following individual and couple reflections using a scale of 1 to 10, with 1 indicating that you need major improvement and 10 indicating that you are right where you need to be:

Individual Reflection

_____ I have an attitude of trusting God.

_____ I spend time listening to God.

_____ I spend quality time each day talking to God and praying.

_____ I study the Bible regularly.

_____ I worship God regularly.

_____ Each week, I take a day to rest and reflect on God's presence.

_____ I have an attitude of serving and regularly serve others.

_____ I talk to others about how God is working in my life.

_____ I regularly seek spiritual support, asking others to pray for me and with me.

Couple Reflection

_____ Our marriage reflects an attitude of trusting God.

_____ We spend time listening to what God has to say about our relationship.

_____ We spend quality time each day talking to God and praying together.

_____ We regularly study the Bible together.

_____ We regularly worship God together.

_____ Each week, we take a day to rest together and reflect on God's presence in our lives and in our marriage.

_____ Our marriage reflects an attitude of serving and we regularly serve others.

_____ We regularly share with others about how God is working in our lives.

_____ We regularly seek spiritual support, asking others to pray for us and with us.

20. Identify several key points you discovered in this reflection exercise.

 harvesting the fruit

21. What is one thing you would like to improve in your personal walk with Christ?

What is one thing you would like to change about your walk with Christ as a married couple?

With your spouse decide on a time this week to review the things you would like to change about your personal walk with Christ and your walk with Christ as a married couple.

During this discussion time, decide on a time when you can meet regularly to have a date with God and with each other. This should be at a quiet time and place where you and your spouse encourage each other and share where you are in your relationship and your walk with Christ.

Over the next few weeks, review the things that you have discovered about one another and your uniqueness as a couple in the course of this study, and spend some time considering what God's purpose might be for your life together. Set aside time for a retreat for a weekend (or at least a full day away) to pray, read Scripture and hear God's direction for ministry in and through your marriage.

22. Perhaps you are already involved in ministry together. This would be a good time to evaluate your participation. Should you continue in this ministry? Should you adjust the level of your participation or your sphere of influence?

23. If you have not yet become involved in a ministry together, use this time of retreat to brainstorm possibilities for ministry. Consider how your and your spouse's unique giftedness, abilities, personality types and circumstances could be used to serve others.

Plan now to spend time on a regular basis evaluating your ministry and listening to God's direction in this area of your marriage.

Notes

1. Victor P. Hamilton, *The New International Commentary on the Old Testament: The Book of Genesis, Chapters 1-17* (Grand Rapids, MI: William Eerdmans Publishing Company, 1990), n.p.
2. George R. Beasley-Murray, *Word Biblical Commentary: John* (Waco, TX: Word Publishing, 1987), p. 272.

leader's
discussion guide

General Guidelines

1. If at all possible, the group should be led by a married couple. This does not mean that both spouses need to be leading the discussions; perhaps one spouse is better at facilitating discussions while the other is better at relationship building or organization—but the leader couple should share responsibilities wherever possible.

2. At the first meeting, be sure to lay down the ground rules for discussions, stressing that following these rules will help everyone feel comfortable during discussion times.

    a. No one should share anything of a personal or potentially embarrassing nature without first asking his or her spouse's permission.

    b. Whatever is discussed in the group meetings is to be held in strictest confidence among group members only.

    c. Allow everyone in the group to participate. However, as a leader, don't force anyone to answer a question if he or she is reluctant. Be sensitive to the different personalities and communication styles among your group members.

3. Fellowship time is very important in building small-group relationships. Providing beverages and/or light refreshments either before or after each session will encourage a time of informal fellowship.

4. Most people live very busy lives; respect the time of your group members by beginning and ending meetings on time.

The Focus on the Family Marriage Ministry Guide *has even more information on starting and leading a small group. You will find this an invaluable resource as you lead others through this Bible study.*

How to Use the Material

1. Each session has more than enough material to cover in a 45-minute teaching period. You will probably not have time to discuss every single question in each session, so prepare for each meeting by selecting questions you feel are most important to address for your group; discuss other questions as time permits. Be sure to save the last 10 minutes of your meeting time for each couple to interact individually and to pray together before adjourning.

   Optional Eight-Session Plan—You can easily divide each session into two parts if you'd like to cover all of the material presented in each session. Each section of the session has enough questions to divide in half, and the Bible study sections (Planting the Seed) are divided into two or three sections that can be taught in separate sessions.

2. Each spouse should have his or her own copy of the book in order to personally answer the questions. The general plan of this study is that the couples complete the questions at home during the week and then bring their books to the meeting to share what they have learned during the week.

   However, the reality of leading small groups in this day and age is that some members will find it difficult to do the homework. If you find that to be the case with your group, consider adjusting the lessons and having members complete the study during your meeting time as you guide them through the lesson. If you use this method, be sure to encourage members to share their individual answers with their spouses during the week (perhaps on a date night).

Session One | A Faith Journey Together

> *A Note to Leaders: This Bible study series is based on* The Marriage Masterpiece[1] *by Al Janssen. We highly recommend that you read chapters 8 and 9 in preparation for leading this study.*

Before the Meeting

1. Gather materials for making name tags (if couples do not already know each other and/or if you do not already know everyone's name). Also gather extra pens or pencils and Bibles to use as loaners for anyone who needs them.
2. Make photocopies of the Prayer Request Form (see *The Focus on the Family Marriage Ministry Guide,* "Reproducible Forms" section) or provide 3x5-inch cards for recording requests. You may also want to have a notebook ready to record prayer requests and pray for each group member during the week.
3. Complete the study on your own during the week. Read through your own answers and mark the ones that you specifically want the group to discuss. As you prepare, pray that God would direct your discussion.
4. Prepare slips of paper with the reference verses that you will want someone to read aloud during the sessions. Before you pass out these papers, you may ask in a friendly way for volunteers, for some do not enjoy reading out loud.

Ice Breakers

1. If this is the first time the group has met together, have everyone introduce themselves and tell a little bit about the amount of time they have been married, where they were married, etc.
2. Invite each couple to share one story of an exciting trip or activity they did together.

3. **Option:** Have each person share the first part of question 1 from Tilling the Ground (p. 12).

4. Before beginning the study, be sure to pray for God's guidance and grace throughout the study.

Discussion

1. **Tilling the Ground**—Ask a volunteer to read the commentary to be sure everyone is on the same page in his or her understanding of occupation and vocation. Invite volunteers to share their answers to questions 1 and 2. Invite the entire group to share their answers to question 3 in order to get a sense of people's understanding of vocation. Encourage individual couples to share their answers to question 4 at the end of this session during Harvesting the Fruit.

2. **Planting the Seed**—After reading Genesis 1:26-31, begin to work through the section. "Knowing God" is designed to help the couples think about the nature of God as one yet three. "Knowing People" is designed to help couples think about what it means to be made in God's image.

    "Knowing God's Blessing" will help the couples to think through the biblical understanding of vocation. Read chapter 16 in *The Marriage Masterpiece* as you personally prepare to discuss the "A Biblical Model" section.

3. **Watering the Hope**—Question 21 is designed to help the entire group have fun thinking of ways to share a vocation. As you brainstorm, let everyone answer quickly and without a lot of discussion. You might want to write their suggestions on a chalkboard, white board or newsprint pad. Then skip down to question 23 and invite discussion with the whole group. Question 22 is for the couples to work on individually.

4. **Harvesting the Fruit**—Explain the importance of making a plan. The adage "If you fail to plan, you plan to fail" applies here. Be sure to encourage the couples to pray together before answering the questions in this section. Stress that each couple may not have a defined vocation during the meeting but that it is important to start the process of defining what it might look like. Part of the work of sharing a vocation will

simply be praying and talking regularly together about what God is doing with them as a couple. When you come back as a group, have each couple share when they plan to get together during the week.

5. **Close in Prayer**—An important part of any small-group relationship is the time spent in prayer for one another. This may be done in a number of ways:

   a. Have couples write out their specific prayer requests on the Prayer Request Forms (or index cards). These requests may then be shared with the whole group or traded with another couple as prayer partners for the week. If requests are shared with the whole group, pray as a group before adjourning the meeting; if requests are traded, allow time for the prayer-partner couples to pray together.

   b. Gather the whole group together and lead couples in guided prayer, asking that God will continue to give them guidance as they share the exciting plan God has for their lives.

   c. Have spouses pray together.

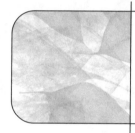

Note: You might want to personally record each person and/or couple's request each week in a prayer journal or notebook so that you can keep track of their requests and check in with them periodically. It is a great way to track the answers God gives them—an affirmation of the power of prayer too!

After the Meeting

1. **Evaluate**—Leaders should spend time evaluating the meeting's effectiveness (see *The Focus on the Family Marriage Ministry Guide* "Reproducible Forms" section for an evaluation form).

2. **Encourage**—During the week try to contact each couple (through phone calls, notes of encouragement, or e-mail or instant messaging) and welcome them to the group. Make yourself available for answering questions or concerns they may have, and generally get to know them. This contact might best be done by the husband-leader contacting the men and the wife-leader contacting the women.

3. **Equip**—Complete the Bible study, even if you have previously gone through the study together.

4. **Pray**—Prayerfully prepare for the next meeting, praying for each couple and for your own preparation.

> **Reminder:** *Leading this Bible study is a short-term shared vocation for you and your spouse. If you want to effectively care for the members of the group, you need to effectively care for your own marriage. Be sure to love one another!*

Before The Meeting

1. Pray with your spouse and discuss how God has been working through your marriage over the past week.
2. Gather extra Bibles and pens or pencils for people to use during the study.
3. Make photocopies of the Prayer Request Form or provide 3x5-inch cards for recording requests. Bring your prayer journal or notebook and review prayer requests for the week. As people arrive, you can do an informal check-in or you can ask if anyone wants to share God's answers.
4. Complete the study on your own during the week. Read through your own answers and mark the ones that you specifically want the group to discuss. As you prepare, pray that God would direct your discussion.
5. Prepare slips of paper with the reference verses that you will want someone to read aloud during the session. Again, be sensitive to those who prefer not to read out loud.
6. Provide blank sheets of paper for the ice breaker.

Ice Breakers

1. Give everyone a blank sheet of paper and pens or pencils and have them write in large letters one word that describes their parent's relationship.
2. **Option 1:** Have each person describe what they most hope or hoped to inherit from their parents.
3. **Option 2:** Have each person share question 1 from Tilling the Ground.
4. Before beginning the study, be sure to pray for God's guidance and grace throughout the study.

Discussion

Note: A challenge in this study is that some in your group may not have, intend to or be able to have children. Be sure to remain sensitive to these couples when talking about legacy. Giving examples of passing on a legacy to a couple's children and to others outside the home will help to keep everyone engaged.

1. **Tilling the Ground**—Invite volunteers to answer questions 1 and 2. Ask the entire group to answer question 3 to help members think about the impact of the marriages of others.

2. **Planting the Seed**—Work relatively quickly through discussion of questions 4-7. The bulk of your time should be spent on the study of Matthew 5:3-10. When reading through this passage, read slowly to give the group time to really experience the Scripture. You may want to help the group imagine Jesus sitting on a hill, speaking these words to them. Give spouses a chance to talk together before answering question 8 and then let them answer as a couple. As you work through questions 9 through 17, be sure to get input from everyone in the group. Some questions, however, require personal answers; invite volunteers to answer those questions.

3. **Watering the Hope**—This section has been designed for the couples and individuals in your group to consider where they are in their walk with Jesus Christ. Read through the commentary together as a group and discuss question 18; then give couples time on their own to consider their walk with Christ. Bring the group back together and give volunteers an opportunity to share. Be sensitive to how God might be moving during this time. Before moving on to the next section, be sure to invite anyone who may have more questions about their faith to talk with you after the study or perhaps during the week.

4. **Harvesting the Fruit**—Give couples time to work through the inventory. If time is running short, encourage them to do this as homework. Come back together and ask each couple to share what one action they are hoping to take during the coming week.

5. **Close in Prayer**—Have each couple pair up with another couple and share their prayer requests. Allow time for the foursomes to pray together and then close the meeting with you praying for the couples.

After the Meeting

1. **Evaluate**.
2. **Encourage**—Encourage the prayer-partner couples to call one another during the week and inquire about their prayer concerns.
3. **Equip**—Complete the Bible study.
4. **Pray**—Prayerfully prepare for the next meeting, praying for each couple and for your own preparation.

Reminder: Be available after the meeting to talk to anyone who may have made a decision or a recommitment to follow Christ. If possible, meet with your spouse after everyone leaves, to pray for each couple individually.

Session Three | Understanding and Celebrating Differences

Before the Meeting

1. Pray with your spouse and decide what you've learned from the previous session. Discuss any changes you have seen in your household since the previous session.
2. Check in with group members during the week through a phone call or e-mail.
3. Gather extra Bibles and pens or pencils for use during the meeting.
4. Make photocopies of the Prayer Request Form or provide 3x5-inch cards for recording requests. Bring your prayer journal or notebook and review how you have been praying during the week. As people arrive, you can do an informal check-in.
5. Complete the study on your own during the week. Read through your own answers and mark the ones that you specifically want the group to discuss. As you prepare, pray that God would direct your discussion.
6. Prepare slips of paper with the reference verses that you will want people to read aloud during the session. Be sensitive to those who prefer not to read out loud.
7. Prepare a game of Battle of the Sexes. Have the male leader of the group think of five questions to ask the women in the group. Be sure to think of questions that might be typical-man questions (i.e., related to sports, cars or tools). Have the female leader of the group think of five questions to ask the men in the group. Be sure to think of questions that might be typical-woman questions (i.e., related to clothing, beauty or decorating).

Ice Breakers

1. Take five minutes to play a short game of Battle of the Sexes. Have fun with this and have prizes for everybody. The prizes could be your favorite candy bar and your spouse's favorite candy bar.

2. **Option 1:** Invite members to share a story that really demonstrates the differences between men and women.
3. **Option 2:** Have each person share their answer to question 1 from Tilling the Ground.
4. Before beginning the study, be sure to pray for God's guidance and grace in the study.

Discussion

1. **Tilling the Ground**—Ask a volunteer to read the introduction. As a group, brainstorm what the basic differences are between men and women. Ask a volunteer to write the ideas on a chalkboard, white board or newsprint pad.
2. **Planting the Seed**—Questions 3-7 are designed to help the couples think about the meaning of the woman being created as a helper. In the past, these verses may have been used to give the impression that the woman was in some way less valuable than the man. Take enough time with these passages to help members understand that this Scripture demonstrates that woman is *not less than man* but a *completion* of God's original intent.

    Invite members to close their eyes and listen as you (or a volunteer) reads 1 Corinthians 13. Discuss the remainder of the questions.
3. **Watering the Hope**—Have couples meet individually to discuss the questions in this section.
4. **Harvesting the Fruit**—If there is time, have couples discuss this section before leaving the meeting. If there is not enough time, strongly urge them to consider immediately after the meeting the action steps that they will take during the next two weeks. Have them pair up with another couple in the group to keep them accountable to complete these actions.
5. **Close in Prayer**—Have the couples that are going to be checking in with each other over the week meet together and pray for each other. Encourage them to pray about following through on the action steps as well as to spend time praying for individual concerns.

After the Meeting

1. **Evaluate**.
2. **Encourage**—During the week try to contact each couple and ask if they have completed their homework assignment and if they have contacted their accountability partners.
3. **Equip**—Complete the Bible study.
4. **Pray**—Prayerfully prepare for the next meeting, praying for each couple and for your own preparation.

Session Four | Living Out the Master Plan

Before the Meeting

1. Check in with your spouse and review with each other how you have been being a student of one another. Talk about what has been difficult and what you've learned.
2. Check in with group members during the week through a phone call or e-mail.
3. Gather extra Bibles and pens or pencils for use during the meeting.
4. Make photocopies of the Study Review Form (see *The Focus on the Family Marriage Ministry Guide*, "Reproducible Forms" section).
5. Make photocopies of the Prayer Request Form or provide 3x5-inch index cards for recording requests. Bring your prayer journal or notebook and review how you have been praying during the week. As people arrive, you can do an informal check-in.
6. Complete the study on your own during the week. Read through your own answers and mark the ones that you specifically want the group to discuss. As you prepare, pray that God would direct your discussion.
7. Prepare slips of paper with the reference verses that you will want people to read aloud during the sessions. Be sensitive to those who prefer not to read out loud.
8. Read John 13–17 to help you understand the flow of the entire passage.
9. Prepare to serve some of your favorite fruits as appetizers for the couples to enjoy as they gather.

Ice Breakers

1. Invite members to share an experience with gardening and especially about growing fruits and vegetables. As people share, think through how some of their stories might help to illustrate the text later in the study.
2. **Option 1:** Invite members to share the one word of advice they remember from their premarital counseling. If they did not have premarital

counseling, ask them to share what advice they received about marriage from a friend or relative.

3. **Option 2:** Invite everyone to share one thing they have learned about their spouse this past week (with their spouse's permission).

4. Before beginning the session, be sure to pray for God's guidance and grace in the study.

Discussion

1. **Tilling the Ground**—Invite volunteers to share their answers to questions 1-3. Encourage everyone to share at least one thing from question 1.

2. **Planting the Seed**—When answering questions 4 and 5, move relatively quickly. Ask everyone to share a response to questions 6 and 7 to get the creative juices flowing for the end of the study. When working through questions 8-13 of the "Bearing Fruit" section, be aware that group members may only have a vague understanding of the work of the Holy Spirit. Take time to give illustrations of the differences between living in the Spirit and following sinful desires. Discuss the remainder of the questions.

3. **Watering the Hope**—Have spouses pair up and discuss their answers to questions 17-20 and encourage each couple to share one thing with the whole group that they learned from this exercise. Don't push them to share with the whole group if they are really uncomfortable, but encourage them to share by your sharing as a couple.

4. **Harvesting the Fruit**—Send couples off on their own to work through question 21. Bring the group back together to talk about what they have learned. Emphasize the joy that comes in serving Christ. Share an experience of your own.

   Invite couples to continue an accountability relationship with one other couple in the group.

5. **Close in Prayer**—Use this time as a way to bring some closure to the group. Pray together with the whole group and have couples pray specifically for the other couples growing deeper in their relationship with Christ. After prayer, take time to talk about what you will do to continue to grow in your relationship with one another. You might want to hold hands in a circle and end with a song of praise.

After the Meeting

1. **Evaluate**—Distribute the Study Review Forms for members to take home with them. Share the importance of feedback, and ask members to take the time this week to write their review of the group meetings and then return them to you.
2. Call each couple during the week and invite them to join you for the next study in the *Focus on the Family Marriage Series*.

Note

1. Al Janssen, *The Marriage Masterpiece* (Wheaton, IL: Tyndale House Publishers, 2001).

Welcome to the Family!

As you participate in the *Focus on the Family Marriage Series*, it is our prayerful hope that God will deepen your understanding of His plan for marriage and that He will strengthen your marriage relationship.

This series is just one of the many helpful, insightful, and encouraging resources produced by Focus on the Family. In fact, that's what Focus on the Family is all about—providing inspiration, information, and biblically based advice to people in all stages of life.

It began in 1977 with the vision of one man, Dr. James Dobson, a licensed psychologist and author of 18 best-selling books on marriage, parenting, and family. Alarmed by the societal, political, and economic pressures that were threatening the existence of the American family, Dr. Dobson founded Focus on the Family with one employee and a once-a-week radio broadcast aired on only 36 stations.

Now an international organization, the ministry is dedicated to preserving Judeo-Christian values and strengthening and encouraging families through the life-changing message of Jesus Christ. Focus ministries reach families worldwide through 10 separate radio broadcasts, two television news features, 13 publications, 18 Web sites, and a steady series of books and award-winning films and videos for people of all ages and interests.

We'd love to hear from you!

For more information about the ministry, or if we can be of help to your family, simply write to Focus on the Family, Colorado Springs, CO 80995 or call 1-800-A-FAMILY (1-800-232-6459). Friends in Canada may write Focus on the Family, P.O. Box 9800, Stn. Terminal, Vancouver, B.C. V6B 4G3 or call 1-800-661-9800. Visit our Web site—www.family.org—to learn more about Focus on the Family or to find out if there is an associate office in your country.

Strengthen and enrich your marriage with these Focus on the Family® relationship builders.

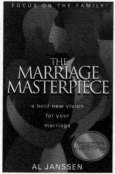

The Marriage Masterpiece

Now that you've discovered the richness to be had in "The Focus on the Family Marriage Series" Bible studies, be sure to read the book the series is based on. *The Marriage Masterpiece* takes a fresh appraisal of the exquisite design God has for a man and woman. Explaining the reasons why this union is meant to last a lifetime, it also shows how God's relationship with humanity is the model for marriage. Rediscover the beauty and worth of marriage in a new light with this thoughtful, creative book. A helpful study guide is included for group discussion. Hardcover.

The Love List

Marriage experts Drs. Les and Leslie Parrot present eight healthy habits that refresh, transform and restore the intimacy of your marriage relationship. Filled with practical suggestions, this book will help you make daily, weekly, monthly and yearly improvements in your marriage. Hardcover.

Capture His Heart/Capture Her Heart

Lysa TerKeurst has written two practical guides—one for wives and one for husbands—that will open your eyes to the needs, desires and longings of your spouse. These two books each offer eight essential criteria plus creative tips for winning and holding his or her heart. Paperback set.

• • •

STRENGTHEN MARRIAGES.
STRENGTHEN YOUR CHURCH.

Here's Everything You Need for a Dynamic Marriage Ministry!

Focus on the Family ® Marriage Series Group Starter Kit
Kit Box • Bible Study/Marriage • ISBN 08307.32365

Group Starter Kit includes:

• Seven Bible Studies: *The Masterpiece Marriage, The Passionate Marriage, The Fighting Marriage, The Model Marriage, The Surprising Marriage, The Giving Marriage* and *The Covenant Marriage*

• *The Focus on the Family Marriage Ministry Guide*

• *An Introduction to the Focus on the Family Marriage Series* video

Pick up the *Focus on the Family Marriage Series* where Christian books are sold.

Gospel Light

Devotionals for Drawing Near to God and One Another